Undulations

Legacy Edition

A Poetic Memoir and Narratives

Eddie Bell

Foreword by Junious 'Jay Ward'
Poet Laureate of Charlotte, NC

ISBN 979-8-88170-017-1

Printed in the United States
Published by IngramSpark, La Vergne, TN
Visit https://www.eddiebell.com

Other books by Eddie Bell

Capt's Dreaming Chair © 2001
Eddie Bell: En Franćais / Selected and New Works © 2003
Eeny Meeny Miney Mo / Time to Lynch a Negro © 2009
Recrudescence / Poems in the Key of Black © 2019

Book design by Kathryn Gantt
All floral photography by Eddie Bell
Author's portrait by Barbara Masterson

For Abraham Shelton, Jr.

Table of Contents

Foreword

The dictionary, depending on which one you use, defines an undulation as the act of moving smoothly up and down, or a wavelike motion to and fro. You may think of waves undulating softly near the shore. You may think of a country road paved into the undulations of a hillside. In either case, you are conjuring both the beauty of nature and the wonder of destination, a journey if you will. When we open a book of poems we want the journey. We want to somehow be seen, but also changed.

I am struck by how at-home I feel in this collection. "Sitting in a country church, Baptist to the bone" reminds me of my childhood, of all the folks in my neighborhood who mattered to me and shaped me. I grew up in a small, rural community so most of us went to the same church. Those meaningful ups and downs on the way to adulthood taught me more than I can put into words. To this day when I think about my relationship to the South, family, and Black folks in general, I chime in with Eddie's words, "I know their strength, their substance, their traveled roads. I join their circle. I am their child."

This is the power poetry wields; preparing a home inside someone else's past. I don't personally know Mama Rut or Gramma Neet, yet I've grown up with them. I must've. Surely Mama Rut bought me an orange sherbert push-pop on the way to the family reunion. Or Gramma Neet ushered me back out the screen door when I came back in the house too early on a summer day. *There's water in the hose outside.*

There are poems here that talk about flowers in the poet's garden. A poem in which he speaks to a visiting Robin. There are also poems that mention or address Sha'Carri Richardson, Romare Bearden, Marian Anderson, and bring to mind magic nights at Birdland. This work calls to the ancestors, inviting their voices into the poems. We are undulating between New Palz and Charlotte. We are undulating between the existential beauty of nature in this country and this nation's sometimes disgraceful treatment of Black lives. There is reflection that reveals both sadness and an everyday kind of joy.

Again, this is the poetic might Eddie Bell commands. I can visualize the poet pruning and weeding in his garden. I can smell the upturn of sod and root and earthworm. I am being cultivated. I am growing. I have learned what you will also learn, dear reader. This book is also his garden. You are a seed.

Junious 'Jay Ward'
Poet Laureate
Charlotte, NC

Preface

Undulations is my most introspective work to date. It speaks to my living in a beautiful, complex world filled with sensual pleasures and societal pain. It is intended to be a conversation with readers and be accessible by all.

Primarily a poetry book, it also incorporates brief personal stories and floral images from my patio garden. It might be deemed unusual to use flowers as illustrators of a poetry volume, but in my case, growing things, particularly flowers, is a passion wrought from considerable time spent with my maternal grandfather, Ellis Garfield Robinson, an Illinois farmer, who passed a bit of his abundant agricultural skills on to me. Friends that know me well insist that I have a green thumb.

The eclectic poems range widely from my relationship with the natural environment to depicting the societal realties of Black life in America. The visual presentation of *Undulations* is enhanced by the inclusion of remarkable work by a diverse group of talented professional artists living and working in New York, and North and South Carolina. Their pieces seen in Ekphrasis are their response to individual selected poems from my collection that I shared with each of them.

As a free-verse poet, who generally expresses poetry in mid-length and longer poems, in this collection I have included a new exploration into minimalist poetry ("Shorts") that tell a big story in as few words as possible.

Walking and biking excursions, ancestor historical reference, contemporary racism, my interconnectedness with nature and my steadfast faith are what inspire my writing. I have never forgotten listening to my maternal grandmother, Juanita Carpenter Robinson, reading her poetry to me while I was still a very young child. She is my writing role model to this very day. When it comes to the foundation of my love of poetry and words, I can humbly say, "I got it honest."

The narratives that conclude this collection are varied personal episodes and historical reflections derived from my living that are best expressed in prose.

Eddie Bell
September 12, 2024

Ekphrasis

'The use of detailed description or an inspiration inspired by a
work of visual art as a literary device.' In this instance it is the reverse.

Kathryn Gantt

Splendor in the Flats of New Paltz

My feet trod the shale of a way through magnificence
An early morning sunrise captured shimmering, ephemeral, spider web sculptures;
and a valley fair enriched by the river, the Wallkill's occasional overflow

My senses awakened and throbbing, surrounded by the waving grasses gone to seed
I marveled at the renderings of God, resplendent palette of nature's full range
The dragon flies helicoptered sharing rhythm with their monarch allies
darting here and there with flitting wings and momentary pauses;
red wing blackbirds joined their silent music floating through the breezy air

Then as if posed for a waiting surprise, Mohonk Mountain appeared in all its
stately majesty
My camera urged itself from my pocket; the moment captured,
a frozen memory held forever

I moved through that vastness of multicolored wilderness, steeped in wildflowers;
a passing breeze cooling my heat-dampened skin
Along the way, a spirit force caused a drift to contemplation of this perpetual
gift of lovely
and as I walked, I uttered a mandatory prayer of thanks
Leaving was the hard part, though I knew it was only for a time.

Barbara Holt

Belonging

It resonates with me, deep with remembrance
Sitting in a country church, Baptist to the bone
The Spirit slowly marching duty-bound to relieve troubled souls
Black folk bringing their suffering and their gratitude to the Lord
Young and old, mistreated or blessed, free or under contrary things
Walks of life of different stripes and colors
God's children on a path to spiritual bliss

It resonates with me, deep with remembrance
The aged deacons front and center;
the weight of praising resting upon their shoulders
Solemn, their voices lifted in prayer and heartfelt song
The congregation stirring, emotions raw with feeling
Solitary congregants proclaiming testimony…
You can't make me doubt Him. See what He's done for me

It resonates with me, deep with remembrance
A voice that can't be silent sings a gospel song
The Spirit moving, folks just can't be still
Bodies sway, feet stomp with syncopated rhythm;
hand claps accompanying the heart-born songs
done the elders' way
Unbound joy, all else of the troubling world forgotten
No highfalutin going on in here
Just assembled Black folk praising their precious Lord.

It resonates with me, deep with remembrance
An invisible mental painting takes me from near to far
From unfree times to present days
To the treasured feeling of being home
I'm in a praise house of slavery times
My body succumbing to the fever in that torrid room
My spirit on fire
Leaves no doubt that I belong

It resonates with me, deep with remembrance
Of those precious people that look like me
I know their strength, their substance, their traveled roads
I join their circle
I am their child
There will always be a place for me.

Cassandra Gillens

Black Mother in the Village
For Angeline Rutledge

Momma Rut. That's what I called her
She didn't mind that shortening of her name
Her door always open; no knock required to come in

She shared her quiet Carolina love so understated and for real
Always welcome, uninvited, sitting happy in her smallish kitchen
At the tiny table placed tight against the wall
I watched her suds those chitlins, cleansing their pungent stink away

With summer's warmth, she planted collards, mixed with other things that grew
It's those little things that made her special, made me want to be around

My days of childhood passed and when I journeyed from the block
I mailed her picture postcards to let her know I'm doing fine
Just my way of acknowledging my love for her; that I missed her when so far away

She's gone now, but not her memory nor the number of her telephone
JA 3-3838 was that number; though now she won't answer if I try to place a call.

John Pendarvis

The Last Flower

The warming air of Charlotte spring brought forth tender shoots,
    my hibiscus awakening from winter sleep

With the rising heat magnificent blooms bursts forth of pink and latent red

Each born to die too soon yet live again, abundant in those that follow

The redeeming sequence a spectacle that cannot last;
    its time ordained by nature's pull

But then in one last gasp of showy radiance it births one solitary bloom
    that briefly sways in the quiet mid-summer breeze

I look deep into that flower and see strength and proud endurance,
    a model for me to persevere, knowing joy awaits the morning

My struggle lasts until my season ends, though unlike this wondrous plant,
    will bloom no more until the trumpet sounds.

Barbara Masterson

Dancing by My Lonesome

Just funkin' like Pieces of a Dream

Down with the beat from the record machine

Swaying and movin'- dancing and groovin'

With improvised steps

One foot at a time.

Nellie Ashford

Truculent Strawmen Posing as Statesmen

Attack dogs pale and whiny came with meanness, disrespect
Ignored her status of being a *Lady*
Demonstrated what ladies like her don't deserve
Black with braids, unbowed and ready
Ketanji Brown Jackson, the worthiest of souls
She withstood the savage onslaught
Heard the unsaid words: *uppity, arrogant, doesn't know her place*
Thwarted at every turn of their savage inquisition
Continued their act with venom so ugly, so unseemly at best
Tried to make her lawful judgments impure; even scandalous
Did not work. Could not break her
Too smart, too measured, too in control
Ain't it pitiful? Their lame approach, tired, though expected
Left her with snarling faces, feigned frustrations
Thundered out to join the others of their kind
But the rational world applauded this fine *Lady*
Made us proud, the ancestors surely agreeing too
We've been waiting for one such as her
Like joy that comes in the morning
Can't no scurrilous puppets defeat the fervent will of God.

Bryan Wilson

The Means for Water

After Romare Bearden's collage, *Noah the Third Day*

Looking at the turbulence, the bleakness of this work returns me to the ancestors
Africans snatched and chained, prepared for transport to an unknown world
Not even in a dream could they fathom what they faced
Nor could they divine that one day, river ships would be a means of their escape
It's the water, the everlasting sea, the ship that courses through the depths

The master's depiction is of Noah; the escaping of the chosen from the wrath of God
An unknown vessel, going to an unknown place of Noah's faith
Excitement of the chosen surely must have taken a despairing turn
Seasick and misery tormenting them among the animals' wails, stink and hiss
What of the thoughts that traversed the family's minds?
No sunshine only clouds and incessant rain
What fate awaited them at their journey's end?
Did Noah calm their feral fears?

Always the water, the water…
Enough to cover the earth they could no longer see
I took no solace for these desperate souls
How could I when all my mind's eye could see was my ancestors' suffering
The awfulness of the slave ship's hold
No sunshine penetrated the depth of the unfree's fear
The consuming darkness, the filth and death
No animal stink, but that of excreta and stagnant pungent air
They, too, surely shared Noah's family's dread of the water
The angry tossing of a troubled, wretched sea
But for the moment I spoke the ancestors' questions I could not hear
When will it end? Does the earth they knew still live?
And will their shoeless feet ever tread that soil again?

Romare Bearden
The Artist's collage *"Noah The Third Day"* unavailable for presentation.

Dreaming A World with Eyes Wide Open

Dreams dreamt in the light of day are not those manufactured in sleep,
but ones risen from the foundations laid by ancestors,
originated by the prophets ancient and wise

Before this poet dreams, my thoughts often travel to the past
chronicling the darkness of those troubled times
Black masses stolen, ridden upon unknown waters
and made unfree in torturous lands

My dreams migrate from past to recent
to unfree hoards convicted by slaving norms
in an unjust land that Jim Crowed, slandered
all, both stave and free
Hell-formed inequality that lowered their odds for living
Freedom denied, hate multiplied
Cast them down to the lowest realm

But life is lived in the present not the past;
should not be as rivers of backward flow
My dreams must build upon the ancestors' dreams;
dreams they dreamt of better days to come

Dreams of hatred dissolved and opened hopeful doors
that bring the light that penetrates the soul,
that changes hearts both young and old
A new world where people see sameness first,
not color, gender, hair, sexual cut or how
they choose to live their lives

Dreams where humanity reigns, violence ceases,
walls no more, impediments removed
allowing life as it was meant to be.

Are these the dreams of a raptured mind
or a prophetic gaze into what is yet to come?
Only time will tell and who shall witness
may not be for the collected us to know.

It is a dark place that I tread;
history's truths splotched deeply in my soul
of those who think me less, unworthy,
who damn me without a scrap of shame

My mind asunder with thoughts of hatred's scale
Entrenched thoughts of malice
Thoughts of kindness shared;
parallel tracks of difficult resolution
A striking back with unholy ugliness
or a kind response that floats upon a different cloud

It is the possessors of tender eyes and knowing hearts
that tip the righteous scale
and brings cautious balance to my existence
and reason to my conflicted heart.

Gramma Neet is Smiling

There was I, in a vast audience seated among many
Not exactly sure why this came to be
Unknown artists being honored
their worthy accomplishments recognized
The MC paused amidst his duties
Looked up and raised an arm to point
All eyes gazed upward, an honorific nod to a queen.

Something unseated me
and up I went to search for the seated queen of song,
Marian Anderson, *The Voice of the Century* regal still
Gratified with her invitation, I entered her box
Told her about Gramma Neet
and her poem written so many years ago
The words still fresh in my older mind,
Lovely like a summer breeze,
Marian Anderson that's you.

Juanita Carpenter Robinson was my answer
to the regal songstress' question
We shared a smile; hers gracious,
mine filled with humble gladness
I left her then, uplifted
My heart never to be the same
And Nita Robinson surely pleased.

March 23rd, Charlotte

Crispness claimed the morning air
The sun bright in a cloudless sky
Lightly layered, I began my morning walk
A three-mile greenway journey
slicing next to the creek named *Little Sugar*
My meandering steps were among others;
walkers, riders, and plenteous dogs
I marveled at the feeling of gratitude that consumed me
The blessing of living to experiencing such a day
Upon retracing this much appreciated path,
the morning so more gently warmed
As my layers thinned, I knew a great happiness
and submitted to a mandatory prayer.

Divination Denied

I sat at the poet's feet, his wisdom parsing the scented air that consumed the room
He sat silent, deep in a mysterious mood, then opened his eyes and spoke a question
What does it mean when old men dream dreams? Episodic dreams that elicit memories
of joy, despair or contemplation?
It was spoken so that he did expect an answer, but only to suggest a thought
I've had these dreams and been awakened from a restless sleep
Ensuing mornings sometimes brought welcome relief,
though the poet's question remains unanswered.

Loss Un-Reclaimable?

The slow slog of time moving ever faster
Has usurped my essence, my memory of things common
Ordinary things deep-seated in past ordinary life
Telephone numbers no longer remembered
Road maps that led me tucked in a drawer
Things no longer done to do no more

Past safety of night time given away to fears
Affordable candy store treats no longer engaged
Baby Ruth's, Almond Joy, liquorish, both red and black
Chuck Taylor All-Stars and double-features at the movies
Cursive and spelling a useful lost art
Replaced by ready convenient machines

Heady technology ingrained in our being
Has made us dependent, less self-reliant it seems
And former ways to do life now things of the past

So onward and upward toward what I don't know
That the reckoning for me will come is unavoidably true
I just hope its forgiving and makes me better not worse
And the good of the past will somehow survive this new earth.

Heat

The Charlotte sun pressed down, relentless
My arms bubbled with sweat; my legs reluctant in their labor
I lifted my cap and wiped my brow
Adjusted my shades for how many times
It was hot and I grieved to be finished
This walk, a dread instead of a pleasure
Then a soundless voice interrupted my thoughts
Who are you to complain about a stroll in the sun?

The voice led me to my unfree ancestors' plight
They toiled torturous fields of cane, tobacco, rice
Cotton and indigo, coffee, no matter what
Deep south sun beating fierce on their backs
Driven like beasts from 'can't see in the morning
Till can't see at night'
Lacking a so needed respite
Limited water the lash their reward
Death the final relief for far too many
It's only God's doing that there were those that survived.

The clouds of the night before parted revealing the symphony of the rising sun. My breakfast made and eaten, fully dressed as rider, I stowed my bike and drove to where the thoughts of the virus and stay-at-home blues were pushed away to a place where I could be immersed in creation. Simple things awaiting my arrival; spring blooming trees, wild flowers too. The cloudless sky in heaven's true blue.

I moved into this splendor cleansed of forethought and worries. The sounds of my wheels on the greenway signaled my movement from scene to scene, carrying me peacefully through nature's bounty so fresh and renewed. Others I passed gave gracious nods, waves, or smiles or friendly exchanges. And so things went, an unforgettable joy-filled jamboree with us living our best.

Troubled in Mind

My brain is burning
Synapses firing in all directions
Making me think I'm being setup for a setback
Life is tumbling, wobbling, straining with what it wants to be
Out of balance leaning left and right
Like a tossing ship whose passengers are not enjoying the ride
I blink my tired eyes as they stare through the fog of time
My troubled mind wondering about it all
The young's walk
The powerfuls' archaic mindset
The vulnerables' lagging will for the struggle
Though the sentient writers write
Wise thinkers think
And seeking readers read
Does it all matter?
Will the stone walls of resistance crumble?

Black Is My Being

(To be read in spoken word cadence)

Did I know I was Black at age two when I knocked on that terrible door that held my dead Mama, when I was told, "You can't go in. Your mother is asleep." That was a lie, because Mama wasn't regular sleeping. She wouldn't wake from her dirt nap, that long sleep of death awaiting the Resurrection and taking residence in her mansion that was in preparatory stages. Was I Black like that 'Little Dark Angel' Gramma Neet wrote about who was late reaching St. Peter's gate? Who spoke his sorrowed apology in native Black dialect?

Did I know I was Black when I slid into my chair at Loves Park Elementary School, a soul dark-skin presence surrounded by a sea of white? Or when Miss Johnson saw my anxious waving hand when she held those few bottles of chocolate milk, a much-coveted delight and didn't ignore my silent agitated plea and handed a bottle to me and not the white girl seated by my side waving just as anxiously as me?

Did I know that I was Black when I was the lone brown face in my Saturday Sabbath School class? Was I aware of it when that woman of the other persuasion flew from her house on our lonely gravel road and smacked me when she saw me teasing a white girl, my next door neighbor and classmate as we walked that country road on our way home from 1ˢᵗ grade when "hardboiled" Gramma Neet, - that's what she called herself - stomped to that cantankerous woman's house, after I arrived home crying and commenced to beating her ass and afterwards being reported to the police and a lawyer friend of Grampa's, not Black, proceeded to get her out of the law's trouble? That woman saw my Blackness. Did I?

Did I know I was Black when young me and my brother, Carl, were ushered into the movie theater balcony in Dyersburg, Tennessee to watch a movie even though we wanted to sit downstairs where white kids were content eating hot-buttered popcorn and drinking Royal Crown Colas from recyclable glass bottles? No, not until we got back home and Momma hipped us to the southern racial abominations, and that info fortified our thinking when Miss Ann from across the street in Dyersburg reminded her that we, her colored children (or did she say Negroes?), should not cut through white folk's yard on our way to the railroad station; our daily path to watch the majestic streamlined "City of New Orleans," red swivel headlight swiveling as it barreled through the Dyersburg train station, not stopping, the ground thundering under our feet and its blustery wind nearly knocking us down?

Now that I knew I was Black, I grew in that knowledge. I learned. I saw. I read. I heard stories and I knew beside knowing that I loved being Black. That I was part of intelligent people strong and resilient. Industrious and talented. Thinkers and shapers of history and doers of art. Survived treachery and still rose amongst the hatred, devaluation, *Jim Crow* segregation and all manner of evil and I too would rise while fighting my instincts to repay hate with hate. Better then to pity than to randomly despise. My intellect tells me skin-color doesn't make people evil, but informs their obsession; their unholy demons of consumption and greed that they do. I am open until I'm closed, accepting until not, together or stay far apart. I'm not what too many suppose. I'm just brown ole me. Confident and equal, maybe better, surely not worse. Some open doors others choose to close. I make true friends or I walk away. I accept righteous kindness and shun twisted hearts. And like J. B., the *Godfather of Soul*, I'm Black and I'm proud and that says it all.

Exposed

Eyes the door to souls… a truth
look deep into Clarence Thomas' eyes
see self-hate /in Black/ revealed

Unfree Survival

Genius … a denied definition
Africans enslaved brutalized restricted
used inborn acumen, ancient secrets, knowledge, to live
put that in your pipe and smoke it.

Solitude

Being alone is not loneliness
It's the absence of a desired familiar that makes one less
the void of friendship and whispered words.

Reconstruction

Forty acres and a mule
tilted words of unkept promises
leaving the unfree to find another way.

Japanese Friends

Yumiko, Noriko, Ta Ke Ko ladies three
full with their culture, heritage, and sweetness
gladdened my heart at home and across the seas.

Proverbial Wisdom

'Everything good to you ain't good for you'
wisdom passed down through the ages
listening ears should abide.

Nature's Lessons

When people are as strong as plants
they will endure and thrive with beauty
like flowers that thrive thru seasons.

Backward Facing Forward Dreaming

I am frozen in a time of progress, out of step with that which passes me by
New words, new meanings, new understandings; a way of life rushing toward what?
A mystery yet unsolved, certainly not a return to simpler times
when truth was not a lie and shaking hands sealed bargains or just a
pleasant moment of human touch

The world is shrouded in bunting, not in honor, but in notification of inclusive evil intent
Or so it seems to me, a modest man of hopes and memories of the interlude between peace and war
birthing a generation of consciousness and love

Oh, to return to those lovely days if only for a minute to relish in things forbidden by the status quo
and gain release to enjoy an air of peaceful abandon

I leak imaginary pleasured tears when thoughts drift back to scenes that never fade;
the pungent notes of Herbie's flute that colored senses in bygone vibrant rooms of pleasure -
named Gate, Vanguard and Playhouse; or Brubeck's passion played in these treasured spaces
of heart throb solos and tinkling ice-filled glasses or a magic night at Birdland when in walked
Sarah invited up to sing a Sarah song

No keyboard stroke of phone and such can match the weightless fall of stylist to a groove,
a true connection between music and motion rendered by a careful hand as sound emerges
faithfully delivering the desired mood. The need to pick and choose by hand, convenience not
considered, the opposite, a pleasured task

This walk of mine through turmoil and desired harmony, a Kaleidoscope of conflicting choices
not all one way or another; an unsafe harbor of haves and hate, compassion or fears
in a world never *really* good to all. Melanin, a curse in the minds of some
Yet the subjected rise and fight through a maelstrom of bitter views of what they've
been taught to feel or understand

As I replay the reels of what rarely was and long for the cutting of binding cords that still hold
captive, the darkness of the underside of human thought and grievance; my feet upon the treadmill
of an ever-steeper pitch. I brush away the bitter pill of hate and pray the voiceless receive their
tongues and the invisible are seen, and a time when kindness is not a struggle, but a casual act
of love

Longing then is a restless toss and turning thing, a backward moment buttressed by a dream,
a quiet storm of billowing sails that when awakened I search for the joy that's promised for
the morning

Life in the Abyss of the Unfree

A backward plunge to the torturous toil of the unfree
house-bound or fielded begs one to ask an unsounded question:
Was there means of pleasure, real or imaginary?
The answer is in their fractured existence
Their route thru pain so complete it surpasses understanding
Yet the ancestors could sing and quilt, cook and create, plant and reap
Love and marry; share intimate moments between man and wife
The sacred appearance of children warm with newborn life
All in the presence of lash and degradation, their lasting enemy
Pleasures taken among the dung of their existence
And even more…
Stolen moments of worship in their unholy circumstance
Pennies earned and saved to yield a freedom
Planned and executed dangerous escapes
Dreams of new life beyond the river
Treasured hope held firm of family reunion.

We're Still Here: A Shoutout to Blackness

Not of our own accord we came
Brought though evil means of commerce
Across God's separated waters wide and deep
But we're still here
Worked to death in southern heat
But we're still here
Raped and brutalized for the slightest wrong
But we're still here
Slaughtered by wanton mobs filled with hate
But we're still here
Betrayed by sorry silver-minded traitors
But we're still here
Lynched in unimaginable numbers
But we're still here
Killed by murderous officers of the unjust law
But we're still here
Shot and killed by others of our kind
But we're still here
Redlined, ghettoed, mass incarcerated
But we're still here

And here we'll stay
We've paid and pay still the awful price
Acts of treachery won't remove us from our rightful place
America is ours born, bred, and slaved
So here we'll stay
There is no doubt.

Runaway Newspaper Advertisement in the *New York Evening Post*

Outsmarted

NEW-YORK EVENING POST.

FRIDAY, JUNE 24

100 Dollar Reward — Will be paid for the capture of my Negro, Edward, he is about thirty years old, medium complexion, well-built, 5 feet 11 inches, and speaks good English, knows his letters and may present forged mariner Protection Papers. He left in Flora Sloop from Charleston May 31 departing for New York City Atlantic Coast seaports. He is a skilled pilot and may seek work on river transports. Above reward will be paid upon delivering him to the local jail or directly to the subscriber's agent. If it can be determined that he is being harbored by any white or free negro, the law will be strictly enforced.

Wilford Southfield Lacy

Palm Sunday Fantasy
After Reverend Ben Boswell's 2023 sermon (MPBC)*

If guns were flowers what a beautiful world we would be
Peace and love relived; lived without unnecessary care
Smiles of greetings instead of fear

If guns were flowers, they would steal the hands of violence
Replace it with a handshake and a positive nod
And bring people forward into extended grace
Would make us glad about living as we run the good race

If guns were flowers, police couldn't shoot unarmed Black men
Children couldn't use them to solve temporary problems
with a permanent solution.
Families would be spared, not left to mourn

If guns were flowers, mass crucifixions of children would end
School would be a place of learning absent outrageous horror.
The treachery of a madden world would be lessened
Replaced by other means than violence

If guns were flowers, bullets wouldn't be takers of innocent life
Streets would become safe, not byways of death
Drive-by killings rendered a thing of the past
The *Hood* transformed by way of God's grace.

*Myers Park Baptist Church, Charlotte, North Carolina

Sell-Out to Beelzebub
Ode to South Carolina

The Senator took the bait, the okey doke
Dislodged his loyalty to the one who made him
Robert Johnson reincarnated; Uncle Thomas in disguise
Sold what was left of his soul for what?
A sly promise, "VP" is yours"... Maybe huh?
Traded his Black (big B) for power that won't tilt his way
God don't like ugly he must have forgotten
He refuses to fathom the promise was a lure
Artificial bait
Now he's just black, (small b), court jester
Bound for has-beenship, mourned and despised.

The Water

(Legacy Museum Montgomery, Alabama)

It was the water, tumbling, rolling, agitated water
The water had me, tossed me aboard the ship
Against my will like the souls to which I lay chained
I could feel it slap against the ship's weathered lumber
The water. The water.
So real. So frightening. So unknown.
My sickened mind and body revolted against the dark
The smell
The moans
What was this thing?
My fear bristled. I shook. I cried
The gods abandoned me to hell
I felt the terror and shit upon myself

It was too real this entrance to the Legacy Museum
That repository of truths
I struggled in vain back to reality after passing through
The surrounding seasick waves
My mind said this was too much and I should leave
But pressed on I did
Walked past the scattered sculpted heads
My ancestors' portraits in the sands
Taken by the imagery of the punishment iron
Born around their blood drenched necks
I cringed; the torture all too real

But it was the water, tumbling, angry that holds me still
The water. The water.
The terrifying water and the graves that it holds.

Live Oaks Silent in the Southern Breeze

"If only these trees could talk"
The words of the garden lady tending the camellias
Beautiful and proud in the depths of the Lowcountry
The mighty arms of the ancient live oaks spread wide and unconcerned
Moss-filled giants hosting the air-sustained plant
They are old, been here four hundred years
Listening, seeing, feeling the vibes
I supposed at night they whisper
Telling what they know
Should I enter among them in the solitude of darkness?
Eavesdrop under their shielding branches
I may hear the rendered unfree's prayers
Rendered away from Marse's listening ears
Steal away prayers of freedom
Blessed by these guardians of the earth
The gracious garden-lady and me in unspoken agreement
When we look at the oaks and silently wonder
What unvarnished truths the oaks could tell?

The floating sensation caught me unawares
But first the walk beside the river, then the sight of Beaufort's Swinging Bridge
Morning's risen sun covered me as I made my way on the concrete path
that held accommodating side-placed swings placed just so
A flawless day of groovy mood and happy thoughts,
though not yet revealing the sudden fullness of what this poem's about

I quit the quiet scene of water, bridge, casual faces
for a stroll beneath live oaks sleepy under a covering of draping Spanish moss
Each footstep taking me deeper into the unexpected clash
The scene so fetching my drifting eyes fell eagerly upon the planter's splendored past
Mansions large and plentiful, lined streets with declarative names…*Prince, King, et al*

Then as if by magic the many, *vying*, ghosts appeared
First those visions of self-righteous covetous planters
Followed by pain-struck ones of the unfree caste
The planters' ghosts wearing begrudged faces, looked,
Turned their backs on me, and marched purposely away
The others, filled with pain, saluted me, and sang a field-born spiritual

Filled with hope, I left those streets with identifying names and balconied dwellings,
those remnants of the trenchant, monied past
Withdrawing from that stately beauty, my mind inflamed with thoughts of sinful retribution

I retreated along my former path pausing to contemplate and reason;
bring new judgments to those unholy times and slavery's reap
of unearned riches and flaunted gain

The day still glorious, the passing people friendly, my groovy mood returned,
but now with deeper wisdom of the fullness of the changes wrought
by the necessity of war.

The Murderer's Rage at the Jefferson Avenue Tops Supermarket (Buffalo, NY)

Crazed young male, a hate-treated loser; a confirmed initiate of a rotten club. After the completion of his evil deed, his membership card was in the mail. White supremacy is what he treasures. Thinks of himself a savior of a non-existence sort. Thinks his lack of melanin a prize. Pale is a lack of color, not a race. Blacks are what he was taught to loath. His mental masturbation a motivating force to take a three-hour drive to shoot old Black ladies, ruin scores of lives for years to come. As his rifle fired did his drawers get wet and sticky? Too bad he deviated from the much-practiced script of shooting his own demented self. Too much a punk to do the sacrificial deed. So now he lives, a ready symbol of human rot until the Grim Reaper claims his due. Escorts his hate-treated child straight to a home in hell.

How dare they!
Dis that beautiful lady,
Marian Anderson,
The one with the angelic voice
That sings to God
Makes him smile as He blesses
I cursed them from my solitary place
After reading and learning of that disgrace
Those blatant snobs of impure hearts
But God whispered to me, said to pray,
Forgive
I haven't
I didn't use the Lord's name in vain,
Though I stilled my outraged voice
And I cursed them just the same
That image of the biddies, their portrait, evil on display
Remains memory-planted in my soul
Pungent with the stink of their evil doing
I'm thankful though that in the end
Lady Anderson received her do
And on her day of grace and splendor
A crowded multitude on those memorial grounds
Were blessed with the heavenly Lady's song.

Wise men with children
teach life lessons … unvarnished truths
that with age are understood.

Karem, brown, tall, graceful, a dunk machine
So worried the suits illegal-ed it
Tethered, he unveiled the skyhook
foiled their crooked wants.

Sorrow comes in many colors
Sleepless nights, crowded thoughts in wakefulness
A listening ear unhearing
Unforgiven sin, judgement, or a failed repentance
Makes one wonder which
Church folk's song peals, *weeping may endure for a night*
but joy comes in the morning
Dismay lingering at sunrise treads upon hope.

Port Of Entrance Charleston
Internationl African American Museum

Sea waters lapped the shore
ancestors' shackles in-place heavy laden
their ship docks at Godsden's wharf.

Shuffler shuffle clink clank
putrid fear sickness-bound sea to dungeon
their journey's end enslavement.

Pools shimmied in quiet tribute
father and son troubled those sacred waters
shoeless purposeful
supremist hate on full display.

The Magdalene's Love Exemplar

Love cannot be crucified saith the Reverend on Easter morn
The truth of that is Mary Magdalene standing alone before the tomb
before the angel appeared and spoke
Love drove her there through tears of sadness
Final act of unhampered devotion
A constant before and after that sacrificial tree

She the first witness of the promise kept
The Master lives!
Her name was called; her practiced love rewarded
Mary, a woman, chosen witness
Not a single man was blessed that way

But that is not the story's end
That same love that Mary lived still fills the world
Goodness and patience, indomitable faith
The willingness of the righteous to do God's work
It can't be smothered
It can't be driven from the land
It can't be crucified.

God said to Moses, "I AM WHO I AM…say I AM has sent me to you." (Ex 3:14)

"You can't make me doubt Him"
Spoken by the elders, their resolute testimony, a witness from their souls
Black Christian folk in churches whose doors stand ajar in the Savor's name
My listening ears heard it sung and said
Spiritual food for a wondering soul
Shared knowledge of the pursuit of those He loves
Me for sure
Know it for myself

I AM is always present
Felt His power when saving me
Two times over, disaster feet away
Words inadequate to explain His mysterious ways
Though try,
Can't keep it to myself

At the edge of a cavern deep and wide
Sure death awaited this camera-bound tourist
Eyes glued to the view through my camera's lens
One step more…
Then a trance-like feeling
His aura gently, firmly, floated over me
Moved my feet to safer ground

He foiled the Reaper's quest for me
A silent, invisible maneuver beyond my feeble grasp
Informed my soul with unspoken words
That it was He alone that rescued me

No matter the prevailing winds of life
I can say those faith-filled words
That simple phrase of pregnant truth
"You can't make me doubt Him
No matter how hard you try."

Human to Human on a Hot August Day

The plump little lady of some age and friendly attitude
Her fair complexion contrasting with my suntanned brown
She and her doggie on their morning daily stroll
Me on mine toward home; hers just beginning
We passed each other on a neighborhood street named Shady View
Our coming and going shielded by its leafy cover
She answered my wave and greeting with a congenial smile
Then spoke her name, Alice, and I answered with mine
Next, her surprising invitation to me, a Black stranger
Who she'd only seen walking on occasional days
Spoke to me with a voice of true concern

     It's so hot. I live up the street, second house on the left.
If you need to rest and be relieved, you can take a seat on my front porch.
The heat, you know, can make you weak and dizzy.

With my soul uplifted from a troubling mood
(This present world will have you feeling down that way)
I appreciated her offer, her unexpected kindness shown,
But I chose to walk on, though now with renewed erudition
That color is not always the great divide.

He, I'm sure it's a *he,* his proud manner setting his tone
         his ruffled feathers a show of his manhood
His first appearance was upon my backyard fence

When I spoke to him — I truly did — he listened
         though he stood his ground aloof and staring
In time, I knew his arrival was an intentional visit
                 knew by his nods and comfortable demeanor
His added song

Each time I greeted him he always listened
         before something urged him to fly away
                 I was not the least surprised upon his return
                         on one ordinary day
Me sitting quietly among my patio flowers

Grounded, he danced a jig with a struggling worm
         then wanting me to see his subdued prize
                 he lifted from the grass
                         flew to a perch, mere feet from me
Looked me directly in my eyes

After I remarked to him my feigned indifference
         his mission accomplished
                 he left me again to my solitude
The poor worm dangling, destined for his mid-day meal.

The Poet's Realm of Beauty

It speaks to the essence of love; a oneness with creation
Looking above the detritus, detecting what is Good
What the eyes can see and the ears can hear in solitude
Mystical and wondrous, a delight for the senses
The whole of it a place where perception and loveliness reside

The beauty of which this poet speaks is arresting, nature in all its fullness
The dewy mist that dresses its floral hosts
The snow parting for crocus clusters in their royal purple and white
The blue of the sky that reveals itself in alternating shades
The mountains in their fall coats of many colors
The wavy crests of winter's newly fallen snow
The birds that make us wish that we could fly

And too, the graceful ballet of haughty giraffes
A mountain creek that shimmers in the summer sun
The silent whisper of a falling leaf
That spectacular sunset that begs us stare in awe
The smile displayed on a gracious face
Two children of different color
Enjoying their playful world
No other care than spending time together.

Lovin' On Charlotte Spring

I'm a spring junky; loving on its annual rebirth
Charlotte's springs a playground for my wondering eyes
High up, low down; all around, a majesty of color:
      white, pink, red, yellow, purple, coming green
A trove of exquisiteness, feast of beauty for the eyes
First one bloom, then another, and another
Nature pays little heed to calendar's stubborn rule
      bursts forth according to its want
I treasure my walks in this early splendor
My steps light, a song of ecstasy throbs thru my heart.

Leap Day February 29th, 2020

This morning while on my daily walk I was accompanied a short way by a winter-dried leaf. It bounced along the curb bringing attention to itself. When it finally came to rest, I waved good bye, a smile upon my bearded face.

The Well-Intended Lie (but lie just the same)

Meant for good by those who speak these words
But foolish is what they are…
'70, 80, 90,100 years young'
'Age is just a number'

You never hear those words from the aged
Used only by the young with misplaced grace
For what they certainly abhor
Youth, to their benefit, are blind to what's to come
And so it is, and so it will always be
Youth is only promised to the young

There's a saddening part to life's old story
Before *getting older* turns to old indeed
There's little gold in those golden years
Though hard-gained wisdom is a plus
The unavoidable fight with 'Arthur' claims its due
CRS, that demeaning plague
Fades our former youthful minds

Pills, doctors, new conversations overtake our being
The fight for life a daily consuming practice
The growing knowledge of what we're not
All those misspoken words should be put to rest
Respectful honesty is always best.

*Can't remember sh.. (*You know the word*)

Jazz Music

The notes flow like quiet storms and rage like fire through dry brush
Heartbeat messages wrought from ageless souls of Black folk born
African heritage and blues foundations
Music born of the unfree's slaving in the planter's fields
Chopping, picking, cutting, reaping
Sorrows expressed of blue times and misbehaving lovers
Soulful confessions of pain, joy and abandon
Miles's muted rhapsodies, Monk's discordant waves
Coltrane's riffs, Brubeck's smooth
MJQ regaling us with sophisticated sounds
Billie's smoke-filled blues
Musician's gift shared by many
For us, for them, translations made their interpretive own
Their stage a counterpoint to mundane life
Rendered rhythms tendered and sweet
Ripe for listeners and mo' better moods
Us tapping our toes or just swaying with the established groove
A grunt or two, muted acknowledgment of Yeah! That's truth
A contemplation
A sensual thing called jazz
Music whole and pleasing like no other.

Thirsty in Colorado

The brother is thirsty
for the City
He remembers the grind 'em ups,
their red lights,
their slow-dragging with
pretty girls with sweaty bodies
He remembers
Tito
and the
Cha
Cha
Cha
Tomorrow
he
will
think about the crowds
and peering from rear windows of subway cars
He misses the mystique of City nights
A sweet flute on Hudson Street
Christmas Eve with Count
Strange he is West
when he should be East
He still wants to step over third rails again
and hit Spalding balls, Momma's broom stick in hand.

The Vaccine and the Woman

I heard her words
spit out with self-righteous indignation
Words ladened with proud authority
a rebuke of the supposed gentry
THEM
The peddlers of known truths
Those deemed by such as her,
conspirators of pervasive lies
wanton intruders taking our rights

I saw her say them
and shook my head
as her words pictured the depth of the chasm
between reality and trust
"You're not putting that in my arm!"
Her testimony that she'd rather risk death,
both hers, yours, and mine
than let her perceived scurrilous jokers win.

Uneven Judgment
For American sprinter Sha'Carri Richardson

Sha'Carri, you're a Black perception, member of a caste
I know that you know. How could you not?

You remind me of Flo Jo
The speedster so dominant, alluring in dress
I'm sure in this moment you're in explicable stress
Denied your access to the Olympics in view
We mourn with you and ask questions too
How could this be? This harsh judgment of you?
They know it ain't right, in fact it was cruel.

The color of your skin is the source of the matter
You're not what they crave, so *they* ignore the loud clatter
The pale men in suits that make these decisions
Black skin and difference still clouds their wide vision
They forgave another's infraction, and did what it took
So a fair-skinned skater could skate
and the multitudes could look

You speedy young woman, too easy to condemn
Mourning your birth-mother's death
Your crime a few puffs from a joint to release your pain
You paid the steep price so the suits could seem fair
No understanding, no margin for error
It's sad Miss Sha'Carri, your misstep so small
That honesty and reason could lead to your fall.

Prophecy

The tread of life lingers, moves through generations before leaving its mark
Minutes pass into hours, hours to days, weeks to months and finally to years

Sometimes wise words take time before a truth is revealed
Young stubborn ears unready to accept what was said

When elders speak, we must listen with intent and regard
Understanding their wisdom will be revealed by and by

The Gone

Long-life has benefits, but unavoidable discomfort
The gone leave us empty, emotionally raw
Somewhat less than we were
Impromptu visits denied by the grave
Emotion-filled talk to remember what was
Recurring thoughts bring smiles and laughter
Fond memories unable to fill the vast void
We must move on with life
It's not prudent to dwell too long on the dead
Life should be lived with hope and persistence
Until the time when our own name is called.

Naming, Shaming or Agape

What's in a name?
Everything; a pseudo state of being:
Negro
Colored
Black
Nigger
Home Boy
Dude
Brother
Frat
How it sounds and what is meant
Depends whose lips it crosses
Inflexion the root
Evil or familiar the intent.

Undervalued
An excerpt from 'Juanita Carpenter Robinson' (Capt's Dreaming Chair)

"Third floor. Lingerie, perfume, lady's shoes.
Watch your step please."
No job for a college woman,
but a job for Nita.
Fair-skinned, fair-haired,
but too black for clerking.
The elevator was assigned to Nita's
old legs and swollen wrists.
Dignified and crisp,
she endured.
"Fifth floor. Men's furnishings.
Watch your step, please."

Old But Still Alive

Hear what my homeboy's mother said,
"Being alive after three score and ten,
You're living on someone else's time"

I'm in that crowd, past 80 and counting
Ancient dudes in the Bible
Lived hundreds of years
We modern-age folk aren't favored like that
Eve's and her husband's tragic mistake
Led to our lowering, reduced our long years
But the Lord in his manner of being gracious and kind
Knew too-long living these days ain't so divine.

Selah

Candy Store Nostalgia

Ubiquitous providers of childhood pleasures
Found memory so precious now lost
Nickels, dimes, quarters even pennies would do
Enough jingling cash to satisfy needs
Coins not just for eating, material things too
On the corners they stood open and ready
To supply daily wants
Now gone forever, assigned to the past
Unmissed today by gadget-hooked kids
No way to miss what they never knew
Replaced, every one, by tempting fast foods
Malls ain't the same and never will be
Can't know our faces much less our own names
We knew we could trust those neighborhood icons
In so many ways
They proffered convenience
And helped make our great days.

Slow Dragging at a Grind'em Up

Low lights, sometimes red, sometimes blue
The basement dark, a preferred state for unsanctioned love,
      physical and imaginative
Social maneuvers among boys and girls,
      both young, and oh so willing
The 45s on the record machine making come hither sounds,
      slow, moving, and sweet
Bodies close, cheek-to-cheek, countless legs entwined
When the record ends, bodies unclench
      heated and sweaty, but enjoying it all
A momentary pause, a short wait
for the next record to fall
It's maybe a mambo or a cha, cha, cha
Some dudes swing to that Latin beat
Others lay for what comes next
Ready to slow drag and cling tight again.

Inspiration

What do you write when you don't know what to scribe?
The teachers will say just write *something*, put some words on the page
I say lay your pen aside and patiently wait
The answer will come
And compel you to work
Because you waited the words you write
Will be the right feel.

Ode to Graciousness
for Mary Wigfall (1932-2020)

My heart beats sad notes to a song that has ended
Sweet song that moved humbly in true graceful living
Showing us what love means and what love does
Now that song is an extinguished melody, brightening others no more

Quietly adorned, the song's singer moved among needful places,
Serving those so easily shunned, so easily unseen;

Mary…Mary, ancient-eyed woman quietly clothed,
Walked this earth knowing life gives reason to do good
Just as her God intended.

Getting Inked

At 79
Old age crisis? Wanting to join the times?
Neither
Just wanting something distinctive on aging skin
A tribute honoring familial love

Mother Dear the words indelibly scribed
Two mothers with differing roles

My skin prepared, the design plastered on
The needle buzzes, vibrates and stings
Then an hour later, it's finished, forever symbolized
My colorful act of respect, satisfaction and cool.

When spring arrives
flowers rebirth in glorious splendor
showy love to watching eyes.

When a friend dies
we carry lonely tears
mourning a life lived no more.

The Black family, not lost or leaving
remains an abode of resolve…redemption
a resilient bond that bandages wounds.

Eighty-four, an age not *just* a number
the falsity spread by the still young
weighs each day and remembers when.

Luther V prayed to 'dance with his father again'
like my prayer… a son's wish to know his absent mama
her touch her smell her face her life.

Beaufort … Lowcountry extravagance
live oaks' giant fingers command the earth
their mossy beards unshaven.
Trees stand silent durable witnesses
to Southern life and gentry
a plesant way to walk and see.

The pink dawn of sunrise
foreshadows what? hope? despair?
another chance to make right the wrongs of life?
or just another day to stumble through the status quo.

Testimony of faith revelatory truths
praise house songs of gratitude for
His steppin' right in when you need *Him* most.

Narratives

❖

How Come My Skin Is Tan?

After my shower each morning, I dry my aged body while standing before the bathroom mirror. The reflected image cannot be denied: less taught skin, brown moles where unblemished skin used to be and even an errant eyebrow hair that matches the consuming gray that covers my dome and chin. No wrinkles though because as we Black folk are fond of saying, "Black don't crack." But my reflected mirror image begs the questions, How Come I'm not black or at least dark brown since my ancestral DNA is West African, the Black homeland where human beings were bought, caught and stored before boarding a waiting ship and transported across the raging seas.

I know the answer though I still ask the question because it is a truth I live with. I know it from the study of dominant and recessive genes. I know it from the tales straight from the mouths of slaves that toiled the ground and kept the master's house. I know it from the octoroon balls where those one-eighth ladies of near-white skin dressed in finery - so pleasing to the planters and their sons - twirled the night away in that obnoxious display of slavery's privilege; a sanctimonious parade of accepted debauchery.

I know it because of the nightly visits to the unfree's quarters where willful pleasures were taken by force, an ugliness that degraded and pained unfree women; their loving husbands Be Damned!

Even with my fractured knowledge of family history, I have to believe that my female ancestors' legs too were forced apart in the dark of night while Master's wife, their manufactured purity intact, knowing full-well when the deed was done. Whether in the Quarters or the Big house, these unfree women were vulnerable and subject to the sexual whims of the overseer and others forced to birth mixed race children.

In my heart of hearts, I wish it were not so for all. That some of my female ancestral aunts, nieces, distant cousins, etc. may have been spared from rape, the back-break toil in the cotton fields or rice paddies and the scourge of rawhide whip under the unyielding southern sun. And maybe like Sally Hemmings, a selected few were granted limited privilege while contending with the degrading state of sexual bondage. It is my hope also that some of my ancestors were able to use their intelligence, ingenuity, and bravery to find a way to break free of the Slavery's evil web and were able to live normal lives of freedom.

My answer to the posed question is to make it abundantly clear why my skin is tan, not black. It is the direct result of the felonious behavior of enslavers blatant sexual desires, in those days past and gone, that tinctured the DNA of my ancestors' progeny and found its way to me passed down through the many generations.

My eyes on rotate, I nervously scanned the West Virginia sky. The dense darkness of the cloud layer over Interstate Highway 81, migrating East was frighteningly perilous. Would I escape the violence that threatened to break loose? I drove on, fear building with every passing minuet. I knew quite well that tornadoes are born in such a covering. Mile after seemingly endless miles I sped along and then like a welcomed awakening the ominous darkness faded and gradually moved westward. The former buried sun slowly revealed itself and the tension enfolding in me subsided and I began to relax. I had made it! So I thought, not realizing terror lay in wait for me and other travelers making our way North. This pause that refreshed was in fact a tease, an impostor fronting for disaster.

The humming tires of my Toyota 4-Runner rolled on as I passed through Maryland and then crossing into the Keystone State, only scant miles from my intended overnight destination. Soon after crossing the border between the states, the speed of the three lanes of traffic slowed from 70 to 60 and finally to 45 mph. What's up? I asked myself. Another accident like the one that brought me to a stop in Virginia the previous day? We plodded along this way for a mile or two then with the suddenness of a switched off lamp darkness consumed the highway and in quick succession, the pounding, twisting, slashing rain, behaving like a madman angry with the world, was doing all in its power foil its passengers' lives and fates.

My wipers, full on, were useless as the relentless tumult obscured nearly everything in my path: plodding eighteen-wheelers, lane lines, exits, and informational signs. Abject fear pulsed through my body as I drove by faith through the midst of this utterly unexpected furious storm. Like we used to say on the Tennessee A & I State University campus when found in such compromising situations, *I didn't know whether to shit or go blind*. I attempted to get off. Not a chance. Should I move to the dangerous shoulder and park or just keep going and take my chances? Only the latter choice seemed prudent, so as I grew more terrified, I maintained my vice-grip on the steering wheel and stalked the long-haul semi barely visible only yards in front of me, hoping all the while that the driver was in control of the situation.

The din of the beating rain and the ferocious wind that slashed against my SUV clashed with the soulful music playing on my satellite radio, so I freed one hand and pushed the off button to end the competition. I drove on like a robot calling audibly on the Lord to save His hapless child. He must have heard my cry because twenty minutes later that seemed more like an hour in mind-time, He delivered me into the former radiant sunshine unscathed though shaken, drained and sweating, but relieved. It had been a trip through hell. The only thing missing was the fire.

Paranoia Unbound

Fresh from navigating the highways from Charlotte, I exited Interstate Highway 80 and into the parking lot of the Holiday Inn Express situated in the wilderness of Drums-Hazleton, Pennsylvania. Nothing around the place, but space. The boondocks for sure.

A creeping feeling of vulnerability slid over me as soon as I arrived. All that I could think of was this appeared to be MAGA country and probably home to some like the 'good people' that violently protested the removal of a confederate statue in Charlottesville, Virginia. A growing dread gave me pause before exiting my truck. Was there somebody lurking waiting to do me harm just-because. Remember the demented white boy that drove three and a half hours to Buffalo, New York and shot ten Black people, mostly old ladies shopping at the Tops Grocery Store. Real time stuff. Could the same evil happen here in Drums, me Black and alone?

I couldn't help thinking about a trip taken with my wife on the rural roads leading to Grandfather Mountain in the high country of North Carolina. Political signs inspired by MAGA littered the lawns that we drove by. White supremacy on display was the vibe that had us uptight. Even sans that signage, this place conjured up visions of our being at risk.

Once inside the lonely two-star inn, the politeness of the staff and their friendly behavior brought a modicum of relief from my discomfort, that is until I ventured out onto Drums two-block Main Street for an evening meal. Everything about the restaurant made me uncomfortable, the only Black person among a pond of whiteness, hill-country folk looking right at home. Good old boys and their ladies is what my vibes conveyed to me. Deep down, I knew that I shouldn't have prejudged them, but a history of similar folks gathering to enjoy a spectacle lynching put me on edge as I waited to be served.

My order soon arrived and I hurriedly ate the piece of overdone steak and a baked potato, paid my bill, tip included, and quickly left. Seated back in my truck, I felt immediate relief, and again when I left town the next morning after eating a subpar Holiday Inn breakfast while being informed by blaring Fox News commentary on the one TV that commanded the room.

Back on the road again the following morning, I asked myself a question. What was the reason that I felt so unsafe in Drums-Hazleton? Was it the veracity of Black existence in our troubled country where hospitable Black worshipers participating in an evening prayer meeting at a South Carolina church were casually shot by a carbon copy of the Top's shooter? Is it because I am an irrational bigot that caused me to react in this manner or am I just a nervous nelly?

As I analyze my own question, I have decided its some of all of the above. I happen to be a worldly person with friends from Asia, Europe, South America, Africa, the Caribbean, and from many different ethnics and political persuasions residing in my home country. The legacy of slavery, Jim Crow and racism though have certainly made their impact on my life, I choose not to live in fear and try hard to judge people by their humanity and not their skin color. It is a struggle to be sure sometimes, like in Drums-Hazleton, especially when it comes to my safety and where I choose to travel, but in general, I trust my better instincts, my vibes, and fight against making societal generalizations. Sometimes I do let situations get the better of me. That is natural I suppose, but I try my best to not let them influence my decision-making process.

Aging – Blessing and Burden

It is a good thing that the full stories of aging are kept from the young. Eating from that tree of knowledge would surely impact youthful thinking about life and its longevity and make them wonder if achieving longevity is a desirable state?

I have reached my eighth decade of living, and to be frank, though I am relatively healthy, well-fed, physically active and benefit from life's comforts, late-life living finds me enduring more difficulties and sadness and less joy. I am a testament of the bleak outlook described so succinctly in the Bible book of Ecclesiastes. Sometimes, things that were gratifying in the past have in the present become *meaningless*. Yet, though I try to move forward in an upward trajectory, doing things I deem significant, I have the constant inward feelings that the world doesn't care. Doesn't value what an old man has to say.

Old people's opinions are too often sidelined and not considered worthy by today's fast paced world that only looks forward to latest new thing, ignoring the aged or even belittling their wise consul. For me, the relentless progress of old age has brought physical decline, mysterious pains that weren't evident when I went to bed and are there upon awakening the next morning. Also, the time-consuming doctor visits as I continue to do battle with trying to stay alive. A new thing has invaded my generation's casual conversations. We have become inundated with the talk of health, ours and our friends and acquaintances. Thoughts expressed of the crippling effects of 'Arthur,' dialysis, joint replacements, cancer, diabetes, and succumbing to our malevolent second cousin, the dreaded Alzheimer's disease.

The worst of all is the knowledge that we are losing, one by one, the friends and family we love. Death, of course, can occur at any age, but it happens much more frequently when we reach our advanced years. It can seem almost daily that we receive that shocking telephone call made by the bearers of bad news. The loss of losing the departed is twofold: an irreplaceable emptiness and the offending sign that our own mortality is facing us.

If you allow yourself to relate to your own demise like I do from time to time, you are saddled with perplexity about the context of your legacy, both familial and public. What will happen with your treasured items? What will be thrown away without due consideration of its value and importance? Who will pass on the meaning and achievements of your life to next generation?

There are, of course, some positives of reaching old age. We have lived to see our children become independent adults and witnessed their evolving lives and those of our grandchildren. We have enjoyed their graduations and marriages and their own successes. And we have gained (at least it's our hope) a deeper understanding of the full spectrum of life. Some of us are unwilling to withhold what is truly on minds and speak our truths without reservation. If we are Black like me, we may no longer shy away from confronting the racist actions of people we encounter in word and deed.

All things considered, I can confidently admit that life is worth the living, but as the slow creep of years that dub us 'senior citizens,' comes with inevitable, unavoidable costs to bear.

The Splendid Grace of Flowers

My relentless fading of vigor and the gradual loss of youthful desires have been supplanted by an intense observation of the wondrous life of flowers. My initial wishes for just adding natural beauty to my physical surroundings have matured into intense witnessing of the quiet strength of flowers. They are models for the way we must deal with things under our care in daily life. Though wild flowers accomplish their independence without our intervention, the domesticated flowers I observe daily on my townhouse patio require much of me.

The extravagant perennials that reward me annually each spring are amazing organisms that cope with nature's rhythms: the frozen earth of winter, the fresh breath of spring, the burning heat of southern summer and the preparation for slumber that comes with advancing fall. Not so the annuals that must be replanted each spring.

Now that I have reached a time in life when retirement frees me from work-related obligations, I spend hours watching the flowers inhabiting my urban garden. I view them in their entirety noticing the smallest of changes no matter how subtle; each new bud or leaf, their change in height, color or fullness. Their reaction to the pull of the sun. I parent them much the same as parents do their children. They have similar needs to be fulfilled.

To help my plants survive, I am pressed to cover them at the dawning of spring when a sudden drop in temperature, a late frost or an unseasonal freeze, threatens their survival. I react to their weeping when they show a need for water. I rearrange them according to their desire for sun or shade. I free them of invading weeds that sneak into their private space to invade what is only theirs. I remove their deadheads to encourage new life and supply occasional nourishment to help them reach their full potential.

With my every determined action, I show them love that they repay with copious splendor day after day. These delightful renderings of natural glory are silent, but their language is known to me and I listen and obey. In my moments of contemplation, they bring a greater understanding of how I should view life. Each of my flowers has a different personality and is unique from each other in assorted ways, even if they're the same species. Aren't people like that and shouldn't we accommodate their differences to help build a more peaceful world?

Dave the Potter is me during slavery or is it best to use the prettied-up denotation, 'the period of enslavement.' He was Black. He was creative. He ignored expected protocol by expressing his thoughts in writing even though the unfree were not supposed to possess that skill much less demonstrate it in public. He navigated the dreadful world presented to him in South Carolina, his place of birth. He was my ancestor by proxy. So how is he me? I'm Black. I'm creative. I have navigated the winding road of Black and white society and have achieved some modicum of public success. Also like him, being Black is very cool with me and I will leave a legacy, as he has, through what I have accomplished through the written word and historic photography.

My elder brother, Carl, accuses me of being a "pro blacker" and on that account he is most assuredly correct. I have been a guest by invitation at the White House, but I live in a cultural Black house. This designation is quickly evident upon entering the front door. Black art of varied medium adorns our walls. Portraits of our ancestral and present families in all their shades of Blackness are there to show from whence we came and what my married union has produced: children, grandchildren, and great grandchildren.

Black books fill bookcases and black dolls (some in the collection are of indigenous Americans produced on western reservations) are on display. Photographs of family, friends and associates cover the file cabinets in my home office. African American calendars secured from museums keep me abreast of the correct day; a needed service of the long-retired.

There is talk among the learned; scientists, writers, and thinkers that race is not truly definable or even that it exists at all. It is a manufactured social tactic to maintain and support difference and class. I am aware of human sameness that the mapping of the human genome has proven. I am also cognizant that color has been a determiner of caste throughout history. How then to consider society race-free (think Obama's presidency) when every measure of human identity is indicated in racial terms. Race determines how and where money is earned, where people live, the quality of their schools, who is elected to political office and who delivers service and whom are the recipients.

I look deeply into what it means to live a Black life as I'm certain that Dave did. We have a spirit of survival by "any means necessary." With all odds against us since our forefathers and mothers were ripped from our African beginnings, we have overcome and prospered in America and at the same time have fallen victim to the curse of white supremacy, Jim Crow and racism and have suffered greatly.

Strong women have been our saviors; the mothers, grandmothers, and aunts, who have raised the children left abandoned by their Black fathers. Acknowledging this is in no way saying that there is not an abundance of Black men who fulfill their role of responsible loving fathers and husbands. Judging from my personal experience, this is the norm, not the exception.

The bedfellows of poverty, discrimination and hopelessness are the result of the strident societal caste system and enforced racial division. Thank the good Lord that with all the compromising negativity Black people face, we remain a cohesive people who love, care, forgives, and supports each other. Collectively, we fight the battles for opportunity, equality, good schools, just laws and against enforced poverty, police brutality and mass incarceration.

I am glad that I have gotten to know Dave the Potter through his remarkable clay pots and the telltale poetic verses applied to them that I was privileged to view at the Greenville, South Carolina Art Museum and by reading a thoroughly researched book* written by one of the descendants of the family that owned him. The legacy of Dave's life urges me to continue to step out of the confines of societal norms and make and leave a record formulated by progressive aspects of my life that others can profit from and be encouraged to make their own contributions to the greater society.

*Carolina Clay/*The Life and Legend of the Slave Potter Dave* by Leonard Todd

The day my anxiety peaked was just before Labor Day in 1958. I was about to leave home and my girlfriend to attend a university a thousand miles away in a place where I had never been. Even though I was a nineteen-year-old young man, tears flooded my eyes that had me wanting to change my mind about the whole college thing. Momma, aware of my emotional dilemma, quietly eased my discomfort telling me, "Wilhelmina will be here waiting for you when you return for Christmas vacation."

A few days earlier, I received a late acceptance to Tennessee A & I State University in Nashville, Tennessee. My footlocker was packed and stowed in the trunk of Daddy's Coup Deville Cadillac along with my portable record player and a large stuffed suitcase. Momma and I stood on the sidewalk in front of our house while we waited for Daddy to finish whatever he was doing inside the house and finally ready to drive me to Pennsylvania Railroad Station. Time was growing short and we had a fifteen-mile drive from Queens to Manhattan ahead of us in the constant late afternoon traffic.

Finally, Daddy emerged and hurried the car out of the driveway and I climbed in the front passenger seat and as we pulled off, I waved goodbye to Momma. To my surprise and disappointment, she'd decided that she wouldn't go with us. I don't know her reason. Maybe seeing me walk into the station knowing I'd be gone for so long would too difficult for her. Momma and I were as close as bunches of grapes on the vine.

Daddy's Cadillac hummed along Grand Central Parkway and we arrived at Pennsylvania Station with only scant minutes to spare. Daddy, being a savvy New Yorker, didn't hesitate before pulling the car into a no parking zone at the rear entrance. A Black uniformed security guard came over to the car ready to tell us to move, but Daddy casually eased him a folded five-dollar bill and he walked away. After parking, we emptied the trunk and tugged my baggage inside and were met by a Redcap that Daddy knew because they were brothers of Madina Temple Shriner's Lodge.

The Redcap attached baggage checks to my footlocker, suitcase, and record player and after another greased palm, he hurried me to the tracks via an underground route to where the silver streamliner was in the final stages of boarding. We were alone traveling this subterranean route under the teeming Manhattan streets. Daddy stayed behind then quickly left to remove his illegally parked Cadillac.

Whew! I let out a deep breath as the Redcap ushered me to my reserved seat. I had made it with no time to spare. The pressure of reaching the station on time was over and that part of my anxiety was put to rest. I relaxed in the cool comfort of the air conditioned coach hoping my footlocker, record player and suitcase made it successfully onto the baggage car.

My ticket was out, at the ready to hand to the conductor as he walked through the coach punching passengers' tickets. The spending money Momma had given me was securely concealed in a tightly folded linen handkerchief and pinned safely inside my drawers. Me and my cushioned butt were ready to endure the long hours it would take to complete the thousand-mile journey to Nashville, Tennessee.

The delightful smell of Momma's fried chicken rose from inside my shoebox lunch, the only thing I carried with me. I wasn't hungry yet and too excited to think about eating the last of Momma's food again until back home for Christmas vacation. My eyes began watering again despite Momma's assurances, but I held back the tears. I still intensely missed the girl that had been a constant at my side all summer: at her house, in the night-lit park where basketballers and handball players roamed, on weekend excursions to our beautiful public beaches and to movies, drive-ins, and church too.

The sudden jerk of the train forced my eyes toward the window as it slowly slid out of Penn Station and away from everything that I was leaving behind. We remained in the near total darkness of the escape tunnel that led to the outside world. A sudden sinking feeling took hold of me as I realized that I was really on my way. And traveling all alone to the unfamiliar place too boot. My only point of reference about going away to college was a disastrous semester at the Long Island university I'd enrolled as a scholarship track athlete right out of high school.

Darkness descended as evening gave away to night and the train rolled on with a subtle movement that rocked me to a dreamless sleep that ended when it slowed and then jerked to a stop. We had arrived at Washington, DC's Union Station. Outside, the cluttered platform was filled with people and redcaps maneuvering baggage carts through the harried crowd.

Still groggy from my sleep, I didn't immediately understand the conductor when he reached my seat and announced that it was time to leave the coach. Confused as I rose to follow his instructions, he cautioned me, "Take your belongings. You won't be returning to this car." Then I remembered that Momma told me that I would have to make a change in Washington, so I assumed I was headed to another train. Bad assumption. She failed to mention the full nature of the change.

I slogged my way onto the crowded platform with my lunch box where another uniformed white man with a black-billed cap like the conductor's pointed me toward the front of the train. I asked him the location of the track of my connecting train, and after looking at my ticket, his reply was, "You're not changing trains only coaches. Just follow those people." I looked at them and saw that, "those people," were all Black (or by the day's racial classification, colored) like me.

Like a bolt of lightning, it hit me. Segregation! Jim Crow! I'd been to the south as a very young kid with my mother and we took the train, but that occurred so many years ago and the details of that experience were foggy and mostly forgotten. I guess Momma refrained from telling me that I would be riding in the Jim Crow coach from Washington to Nashville because she feared that might be a deal breaker.

Prior to the time Momma convinced me that it was time to go back to college again, I'd been in a deep funk resonating from my previous college experience where a profoundly negative racial experience drove me away from that predominately white Long Island university. In the aftermath of my absconding without bothering to do anything official, I dealt with it by running away from my St. Alban's home and back to my grandparents' house in Loves Park, Illinois. That's a story for another time.

I reached the designated coach and dragged myself and my lunch into a scene resembling something out of an old west movie. It was coach filled with mostly other Black kids that I soon discovered were also on their way to southern Black colleges. The luxurious appointments of my previous coach were absent. Though my daddy paid for a first-class ticket, I was deposited in third-class accommodations of a degraded relic. A stark difference from the coach I boarded in New York City.

Slowly I began to take in my surroundings, a coach filled with kids that looked like me, but still unfamiliar since I didn't know any of them. Some looked several years older than me and others similar in age. I felt lost, a stranger in a world I did not know. I had no desire to mix. I just wanted to be left alone. I did respond to the question put to me by a boisterous dude that wanted to know my college destination. My answer, "Tennessee A & I," resulted in his public announcement that I was a newbie freshman. He said it in such a manner that made my uneasiness only worse. What was I going to face when I reached campus? The kids near me hooped and hollered shook their heads as if they were sorry for my upcoming fate.

Eventually things quieted down and soon I was forgotten. After the train began moving again the kids move into their separate groups and carried on like they were having a party. The seats in the coach could be shifted to face each other and lots of them took advantage of that feature.

Gradually, as the train traveled through obscure little towns, at some of which it made brief stops. I slowly came to the realization that entering a new world might not be so bad. I was among more Black students all in one place that I'd ever been. Throughout my twelve years of education, I'd not only never had a Black teacher, I was rarely in a high school class with more than one or two other Black students. Many times, there were none.

My St. Albans neighborhood eventually turned all-Black, except for Mrs. Thompson, the wife of the block's watchdog. My Loves Park, Illinois Elementary School first grade class was all-white except for me. Point of fact, I was the only Black kid in the whole school! At the time I was living with my grandparents in Loves Park, where we were the only Black family. PS 36, my St. Albans Elementary School, was mostly white, but several Black kids from my neighborhood also attended.

Riding in that segregated train coach for so many hours, in a way, began to feel like I was with extended family. The segregation put upon us in that frazzled coach was meant to keep us in our divided racial place. It was an enforcement of the rules of the racial caste system that mandated *coloreds* must be separated from whites, except to serve and entertain them. I began to realize that I didn't care. Riding in that Jim Crow coach had, in effect, introduced me to a new joy that would soon consume me. Other than my immediate friends and family, I had always been surrounded by white people. Now that I was going to a Black college, an HBCU, where I would, at last, be in the majority, was a positive change. That universe of Black would set me on a course of oneness with my people and a richness that would make me whole.

The Jim Crow train was an evil gesture to force us beneath our dignity and our rights, though at the same time it ignited a fire in me to get to know and experience the full Black way of living. Tennessee State embraced me. At the beginning of my journey to the South, I was only looking forward to running track, making a satisfactory adjustment to my new college, and coming back home at Christmas to reunite with my girlfriend. Nothing more. In the coming days and months though that thinking changed dramatically. It was the time of sit-ins and the Civil Rights Movement. I became deeply acquainted with the struggle for equality and aware of the sacrifice that required. I grew up during those four years. I released my inner Blackness and enjoyed the experience. It was a life-changing adventure.

Acknowledgments

Special thanks to Anthony Hartis of Digital Control Company, Charlotte, North Carolina, for his excellent camera work copying and digitizing three of the artist's paintings that appear in the Ekphrasis section of the book.

My heartfelt thanks to Kathryn Gantt of Paragon Studios, Charlotte, North Carolina, for working closely with me throughout the entire process. Her thoughtfulness and graphic design creativity have produced a visually appealing book that is easy to read. In truth, she has been more than just a designer, but also a friend, who has worked tirelessly tending to all the many details of bringing the book to fruition. She is a Godsend to me.

And to my wife, Wilhelmina, for supporting me throughout as reader of the manuscript and a companion and motivator. She has even selected one of the poems in the collection to be read at her Homegoing Service.

Artist Credits

Nellie Ashford

Charlotte native, Nellie Ashford is a folk artist whose work expresses cultural identity, shared community values and aesthetics. Inspired by the life that surrounds her and memories of her past, Ashford's work incorporates a mix of materials that often reflect real-life experiences and depicts families, children, dancers and musicians with vibrant detail and emotion. Each work that she creates has a story to tell. Vintage fabrics, cloth images of people who reflect varying ethnic, religious, occupational, age and gender identities. They identify and complement each other and their world. Nellie Ashford is an untold jewel, and it is through her art that she creates a world of historical expression – a visual, realistic imagery that reflects a time gone by, allowing the viewer to reflect and understand the Charlotte that once was – her Charlotte. Her work has been exhibited throughout the Carolinas, The Mint Museum and The Levine Museum of the New South.

Cassandra Gillens

Cassandra Gillens is a self-taught artist. Her earliest memories of drawing with colored pencils in Roxbury, Massachusetts remained a part of her when she began to paint pictures depicting her early childhood years. Her fondest memories of her visits to South Carolina moved her to paint these visions of the Lowcountry's comforting southern culture. Upon her return, she became closely connected with her people and culture she so loved. Cassandra's paintings show that love with vivid colors of the southern seasons and images of good old southern living. Her art can be found in all parts of the Lowcountry, and various states throughout America.
Cassandragillensarts.com

Barbara Holt

I am an artist who has created in many styles, techniques, and mediums over a long period of time. I have a BFA in Painting from the School of Visual Arts, and an MFA in Painting from SUNY New Paltz. I've also studied at the Woodstock School of Art and the Boca Raton Museum School. Teaching Art at many levels for thirty years in NYC and upstate brought me many new experiences, but kept me from a full-time pursuit of my own artistic path. In retirement, I live and maintain a studio in the Mid-Hudson Valley in the Town of New Paltz, New York. I frequently travel to California and Florida and utilize those landscapes as inspiration in my paintings. My paintings have been in group and solo exhibitions, including NYC, Florida, and the Hudson Valley. My expressions in Fine Art are gaining momentum and focus now that I am retired from Art Education.
BarbaraHoltart.com

Barbara Masterson

Art is like a serum, transforming its audience for good or ill. Familiar shapes in
fields, migrant workers toil in the Hudson Valley doing jobs most Americans won't. Who
are they? Can you see them? It's possible for society to confer invisibility on a group.
What role do we play in keeping them unseen? My work can expand our perceptions of
these workers. If only by their images in my paintings, the viewer will come to see these
persons for the vital role they have in our lives.
Barbaramasterson.com

John Pendarvis

Pendarvis is a native South Carolinian, whose works include collages, mixed media
canvases, serigraphs and paper pieces. He studied with Leo Twiggs at S.C. State
University, Arts Student's League, New York City and Museum School of Art, Greenville
County Museum with Carl Blair. I like using my hands, brushes, knives, and other objects
to create. My art is a celebration of life inspired by a love of music, the outdoors, my
culture and exploration. It's about opening your eyes and allowing yourself to be taken on
a journey.
JohnPendarvis.com

Bryan Wilson

Bryan Wilson grew up between New Jersey and Georgia. It was in Georgia, at the
age of 16, that he began his artistic career. He graduated Magna Cum Laude with
a BA in Studio Art with a Minor in Graphic Design from Morris Brown College.
After graduating college, he became an in-house Graphic Designer for the Center
for Puppetry Arts in Atlanta, GA. After a couple years, and getting married, he and
his wife relocated to Charlotte, NC, where he began teaching art at a public school
and obtained his teaching credentials at University of North Carolina-Charlotte.
It was in 2012 that Bryan decided to take his painting, and picture-making ability
to another level by pursuing his MFA in Drawing/Painting at the Academy of Art
University where he graduated in 2015. He is now exhibiting throughout the US
and abroad alongside other distinguished artists.
www.bryanwilsonstudios.com

Eddie Bell

Eddie Bell is an eclectic writer, poet, photographer, educator, and world-traveler. Dubbed a 'renaissance man,' he has collaborated visual artists, videographers and a classical violinist, as well as jazz musicians with the goal of adding dimension to his poetry. His earlier works have been translated into French and Russian. *Undulations* is his fifth poetry collection. He is a New Paltz, NY transplant currently residing in Charlotte, North Carolina.

www.eddiebell.com
Email: eddiebellink@gmail.com